The Water Cycle

The Water Cycle

Trudi Strain Trueit

Franklin Watts
A Division of Scholastic Inc.
New York • Toronto • London • Auckland • Sydney
Mexico City • New Delhi • Hong Kong
Danbury, Connecticut

To my dad, Dean Strain, for providing me with the essentials: undying faith, love without limits, and peanut butter

Note to readers: Definitions for words in **bold** can be found in the Glossary at the back of this book.

Photographs ©: Archive Photos: 38 (Petar Petrov/Reuters), 43 (Sukree Sukplang/Reuters); Corbis-Bettmann: 18 (AFP), 35 (Carol Cohen), 25 (Roman Soumar), 41 (The Purcell Team), 2 (Nik Wheeler); Dembinsky Photo Assoc.: 14 (G. Alan Nelson), 31; Liaison Agency, Inc.: 40 (Georges De Keerle/DaimlerChrysler/Newsmakers); NASA: 9 (USGS); Peter Arnold Inc.: 5 left, 15 (S.J. Krasemann), 36 (Ray Pfortner); Photo Researchers, NY: 8 (Jim Corwin), 10 (Bernhard Edmaier/SPL), 5 right, 28 (Douglas Faulkner), 22 (G. Brad Lewis/SPL), 17 (Will & Deni McIntyre), 23, 24 (NASA/SPL), 33 (David Parker/SPL), 12 (Alfred Pasieka/SPL); Stock Boston: 45 (Robert Caputo); Stone: 6 (Paul Dance), cover (Ernst Haas); The Image Works: 39 (Townsend P. Dickinson), 46 (L. Kolvoord), 26 (Sean Ramsay); Visuals Unlimited: 16 (John Gerlach), 20 (Ernest Manewal), 32 (Bernd Wittich).

The photograph on the cover shows raindrops on a leaf. The photograph opposite the title page shows the Nile River in Aswan, Egypt.

Library of Congress Cataloging-in-Publication Data

Trueit, Trudi Strain.
    The water cycle / Trudi Strain Trueit.
        p. cm.— (Watts Library)
    Includes bibliographical references (p.).
    ISBN 0-531-11972-6 (lib. bdg.)   0-531-16220-6 (pbk.)
    1. Hydrologic cycle—Juvenile literature. [1. Hydrologic cycle. 2. Water supply.] I. Title. II. Series.
GB848 .T78 2001
551.48—dc21   2001017576

Contents

Almost all the water on Earth—including the tear dropping from this woman's eye—has been around for more than four billion years.

Chapter One

The Never-Ending Journey

Would it surprise you to discover that the ice in your glass of lemonade was once a snowflake? How about if the tears in your eyes were, long ago, drops in a pool where dinosaurs came to drink? Well, both are possible. Nearly all of the water on Earth is the same water that has been here since our oceans formed more than four billion years ago. Each raindrop and

Space Water

Once in a while, an icy comet enters Earth's atmosphere and breaks apart, bringing some new water to a very old cycle.

Together, the five oceans contain 97 percent of Earth's water. Here, waves break against rocks along the Pacific coast in the state of Oregon.

snowflake that falls is on an endless path from the sky to the ground (or ocean) and back to the sky again. This loop is called the **hydrologic cycle**, or water cycle.

Each drop of water takes a unique path on its quest. For instance, if a drop falls into a river, it might stay there for three weeks. If it touches down in a glacier, it could remain frozen for hundreds of years. If it sinks into the soil, the drop could be trapped underground for as long as forty thousand years. Eventually, though, all water that falls finds its way back up into the air to keep the cycle going.

Blue World

There are about 340 million cubic miles (1.5 billion cubic kilometers) of water on Earth. To picture this, imagine the United States as a swimming pool 100 miles (160 km) deep,

Is Anyone Out There?

For years, scientists believed that Earth was the only planet in our solar system with water and, therefore, with living organisms. Recently, NASA's *Galileo Probe* discovered ice on Europa, one of Jupiter's moons. Could life exist there, too? Maybe. The *Mars Pathfinder* and *Global Surveyor* have found water in the form of polar ice caps and faint vapor **clouds**, and there is some evidence of springs flowing less than 1 mile (1.6 km) underground. Although the atmosphere on Mars is too cold for liquid water to exist on the planet's surface today, satellite images show canyons carved into the red planet—signs that rivers might have flowed on Mars billions of years ago.

coast to coast. At any given moment, 97 percent of all our water is flowing in the seas. Earth's oceans—the Atlantic, the Pacific, the Indian, the Arctic, and the Antarctic—cover 71 percent of the planet's surface.

Three percent of Earth's water supply is fresh, but 2 percent of that amount is trapped in ice at the North and South Poles. The remaining freshwater flows in rivers, lakes, and under the ground. It is this small amount—less than 1 percent—that must provide all the world's freshwater.

Opposite: *Two-thirds of the world's freshwater supply is frozen in glacial ice. Pictured here is the Gilkey Glacier in Alaska.*

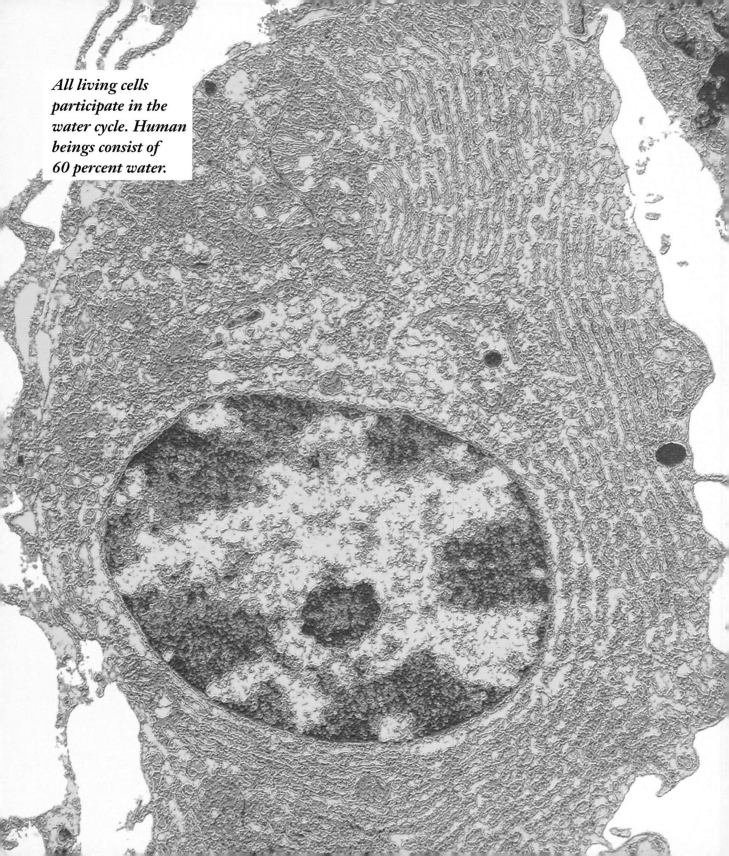

All living cells participate in the water cycle. Human beings consist of 60 percent water.

Chapter Two

Water in Motion

From Africa's Kalahari Desert to the Amazon Rain Forest in South America, every living cell in every living being needs water, including you. You can survive for about a month without food, but you would not last more than a week without water. Humans are 60 percent water. Your body needs 2 quarts (about 2 liters) of water each day.

Just what is this nearly colorless, odorless, and tasteless fluid we cannot do without? A **water molecule** (H_2O), the

See-through Seas?

Water is either clear or tinted slightly blue. Deep ocean water gets its color by reflecting the most intense color of the Sun: blue. Plants, minerals, soil, and pollutants also affect the sea by painting it various shades of blue, green, or even black.

On the Bear Island River in Minnesota, ice forms as water molecules slow down.

smallest particle of water, is made up of two hydrogen atoms and one oxygen atom, which are too small to see even under a microscope. It takes about ten billion molecules to make just one droplet of water.

Water molecules are constantly racing around and tumbling over each other, which is why water does not keep a constant shape. Change the temperature, however, and the molecules change, too. If you place water in the freezer, the molecules begin to slow down. When the temperature lowers to 32° Fahrenheit (0° Celsius), the **freezing point** of water, the molecules slow down so much that they turn into a solid: ice.

Heating water molecules breaks their bonds and causes them to **evaporate**, or turn from a liquid into a gas. Watch a wet sidewalk dry up on a sunny day, and you are seeing how the warmth of the Sun causes water to change into an invisible gas called **water vapor**. You cannot see, smell, or taste this gas, but if you have ever been sticky on a summer's day, you have certainly felt it.

Humidity, the amount of water vapor in the air, is usually expressed as a percentage. One hundred percent relative humidity means the air is holding all the moisture it can hold (not that it is raining). On a hot July day, humid air feels heavy or muggy. At any given moment, there are about 25 million pounds (11 million kilograms) of water vapor in the air. If it all turned into rain and fell at once, the entire world would be covered in 1 inch (2.5 centimeters) of water.

Triple Duty

Water is the only substance on Earth that exists in three forms: solid (ice, hail, and snow), liquid (rain and dew), and gas (water vapor).

Water on the Rise

When sunlight warms pockets of water vapor near the ground or over the ocean, the gas begins to rise and cool down. The vapor latches onto tiny particles of dust, dirt, pollen, or salt in the air. These particles, called **cloud condensation nuclei (CCN)**, help water vapor to **condense**, or turn from a gas into a liquid. As the vapor condenses, clouds begin to form.

If temperatures within the cloud are below freezing, the vapor condenses not as droplets but as ice crystals. The tiny droplets or crystals collide, combine,

Water condenses around particles in the air to form clouds. When the droplets get too heavy, they fall. Here, rain pours from clouds in Africa.

and grow. When the crystals or drops get too heavy for the cloud, they come down as **precipitation**—any liquid or solid water that falls from the sky. Crystals form snowflakes, while water droplets become raindrops.

Water vapor that rises from the ocean leaves its salt behind and begins the cycle again as freshwater. If the fresh drops happen to fall in the ocean, they become part of the salty seas once again. About 80 percent of Earth's precipitation falls into the oceans.

In one day, a birch tree releases about 70 gallons (265 L) of water into the air in a process called transpiration.

Perspiring Plants

Another way water vapor seeps into the atmosphere is through the leaves of plants. Groundwater is absorbed by a plant's roots, rises through the stem, enters the leaves, and then **transpires**, or evaporates, through tiny openings called **stomata**. In one day, a sunflower releases nearly 2 pints (1 L) of water into the air, while a birch tree "sweats" off about 70 gallons (265 L).

Since most plants are about 90 percent water, they must keep drawing liquid into their roots to make up for water lost through transpiration. Some plants, such as those in the desert, live on small amounts of water, so they cannot afford to transpire much vapor. That is why cacti adapted thorns—smaller,

16

In the thick vegetation of rain forests, such as this one in Brazil, transpiration accounts for up to half the regional rainfall.

modified leaves that keep the plant from sweating away valuable fluids.

Eighteenth-century scientist Stephen Hales discovered that plants move so much water from the ground to the air that they can have a major impact on weather. In a tropical rain forest, where it rains more than 80 inches (200 cm) per year, plant transpiration can account for as much as half the annual rainfall. You might say a rain forest helps make its own rain!

Drip Trip

A water molecule spends about eight to ten days in the air between evaporation and precipitation.

17

Soldiers inspect the flood-ravaged barrio of San Bernardino in Caracas, Venezuela, in December 1999.

Chapter Three

Forces of Nature

As billowy gray clouds tumbled overhead and the first drops dampened the earth, no one in Venezuela predicted that one of the worst natural disasters of the twentieth century was about to happen. During several days in December 1999, heavy rains pounded northern sections of South America. Mountains became so saturated that they crumbled like wet sand castles. Massive mudslides washed away entire towns and villages. By the time the storms ended two weeks later, thirty thousand people had died and seven thousand were missing. Scientists estimated that the storms dumped nearly 20 inches (50 cm) of rain on Venezuela—ten times the normal amount for that time of year.

Too much rain can be disastrous, but too little can be equally scary. At almost the same time that floods were drenching South America, farmers in Mexico wondered if they would ever see a drop of rain again. Day after blistering day, the scorching 100° F (38° C) heat wave shriveled crops and killed cattle. The Rio Grande, the river that forms the U.S.-Mexico border, had run dry along one stretch. Some

A drought period can have as horrible an impact on human life as flooding does. Here, a section of the Rio Grande runs almost dry.

farmers were watering their fields with raw sewage just to keep their crops alive. It was the second straight **drought** year for Mexico, where, in some places, rainfall was 90 percent below normal.

How is it that one place can receive so much precipitation while another gets barely a drop? The answer lies in the major forces of nature that control our water cycle. The Sun, the **winds**, and the ocean currents work together to determine where, when, and how water will fall on Earth.

Sun Reign

It is the Sun's heat, or energy, that keeps the water cycle in motion. Sunlight provides our atmosphere with as much energy as 200 million electric power plants. This energy warms the land and oceans to create water vapor, precipitation, and winds.

Oceans are like storehouses for the Sun's energy. By soaking up heat, water cools the Earth and regulates its temperatures. Water absorbs so much energy that scientists believe the top 10 feet (3 meters) of the oceans contains as much heat from the Sun as Earth's atmosphere does.

Oceans help regulate temperatures on Earth by soaking up the heat of the Sun.

Because Earth's surface is curved, some places around the globe receive more intense heat than others. Areas near the equator, which receive the most direct sunlight, are the hottest. They are also the wettest, since warm, moist ocean air churns up more storms than cooler air does. In contrast, the North and South Poles, farthest from the Sun, are the coldest and driest spots.

Blowing Breeze

If you have ever felt a cooling breeze on a spring day, you know the air around us is always moving. When air circulates around the globe, it is called wind. You might not be able to feel it, but the atmosphere is constantly pressing down on us with a force of about 15 pounds per square inch (1 kg per square cm). **Atmospheric pressure,** the weight of air, is what makes your ears pop when you go up (or down) in an elevator. It also helps drive Earth's winds.

The Sun heats air near land, oceans, and mountains differently. Warm, rising air creates high-pressure areas, while sinking, cooling air causes low pressure. Air constantly moves from warm areas of high pressure to cool areas of low pressure. The greater the temperature difference from one area to another, the harder the wind blows.

Big bands of winds called **prevailing winds** continually circle the planet. These winds, such as polar easterlies, westerlies, and trade winds, tend to blow from a particular

This satellite map shows wind speed and direction over the Pacific Ocean. Arrows show direction, and colors refer to speed. Blue indicates wind speeds of 0–9 miles per hour (0–14 kph); purple and pink, 10–27 mph (15–43 kph); and red and orange, 28–45 mph (44–72 kph).

Grand Slam

Want to hit a home run? Your best bet is Coors Field in Denver. Higher elevations have lower air pressure, or fewer air molecules in a given space. Since there is less air resistance, a baseball flies a bit farther in the Mile High City than it does in most other ballparks.

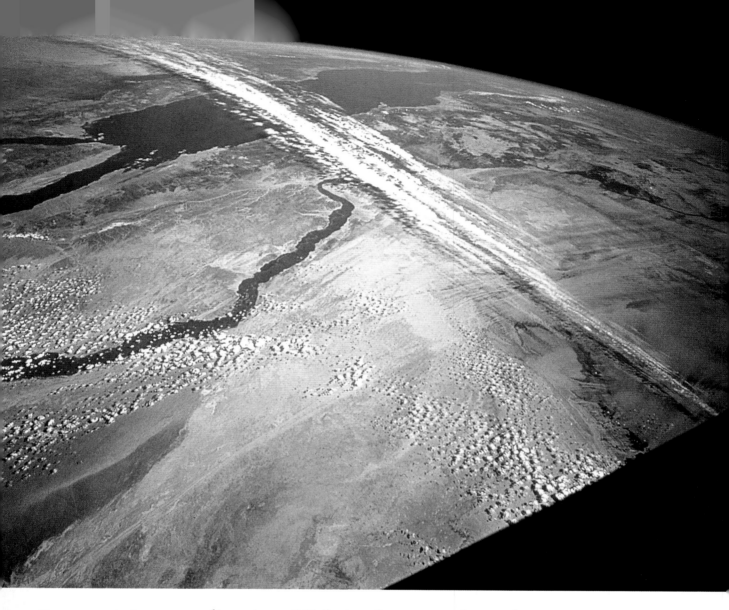

Jetstream winds blow a trail of clouds across the atmosphere over Egypt.

direction. High in the atmosphere, between 20,000 and 40,000 feet (6,100 and 12,200 m), differences in pressure and temperature create strong winds called **jetstreams**. Within jetstreams, wind speeds can top 200 miles (320 km) per hour. Jetstreams blow major storms around the globe from west to east.

By moving clouds and storms across the sky, winds affect where rain falls on our planet. For instance, a wind called the Pineapple Express can drive warm, wet air all the way from Hawaii to the mainland United States. This flow brings plenty of rain, along with unusually warm winter temperatures, to the Pacific Northwest.

Flowing Seas

Just as winds affect **climate**, so do the oceans. Ocean currents carry warm and cold waters great distances. These currents can change sea-surface temperatures, which, in turn, help shape Earth's climates. The warm Gulf Stream, for instance, carries warm water from the equator up the east coast of the United States to northern Europe. Without this band of warm water, these regions would have much lower temperatures.

A woman and her child walk in heavy rain in Bali. Warm ocean currents bring moist air—and high levels of rainfall—to tropical countries.

El Niño's Touch

Scientists are just beginning to learn about an ancient weather wonder called **El Niño**, a slight shift in ocean currents that affects the delicate balance of the world's water cycle. Normally, warm waters flow in the western Pacific Ocean near Australia, while waters are cooler in the eastern Pacific near South America. About once or twice a decade, the trade winds that push the cold ocean currents weaken, die, or even reverse. The warm waters from Australia begin to flow eastward, blocking the cold waters from their usual path up the coast of South America. Several hundred years ago, fishermen near Peru noticed this change. They called it El Niño, referring to the baby Jesus, because it often arrived near Christmas.

El Niño can be a welcome sight or an unwanted guest. Here are just a few of its seesaw results:

- Heavy rains soak the west coasts of the United States and South America, while northern regions of the United States and Canada enjoy mild and dry winters.
- Anchovies and sardines that migrate with nutrient-rich cold water never make it to Peru, and some commercial fishermen lose their jobs.
- The Atlantic gets far fewer hurricanes, while the Pacific churns up many more storms than usual.

Our seas provide plenty of water vapor to create clouds and storms. The warm, moist air that comes with warm currents causes increased precipitation in countries near the equator, while cold and inland regions get far less rain. Tropical rain forests near the warm waters of the equator get anywhere from 80 to 200 inches (200 to 500 cm) of rain per year, while the frigid poles receive only a few inches of snow each year.

Scientists are continually mapping ocean currents. In 1990, their research got a rather unusual helping hand. A Korean cargo ship bound for the United States accidentally dumped eighty thousand athletic shoes into the Pacific Ocean. Over the years, the sneakers have been found on shorelines from Alaska to Oregon to Hawaii, giving oceanographers valuable information about the flow of our ocean currents.

On its way to the ocean, the Colorado River continually carves out the Grand Canyon in Arizona.

Chapter Four

Sea to Sky to You

Water is constantly shaping and reshaping the surface of our planet. **Runoff**, precipitation that does not soak into the ground, **erodes**, or cuts into, the land. Over time, rivers, glaciers, and other types of **surface water** carve out canyons and valleys as the water makes its way back to the sea. The Grand Canyon in Arizona is a good example of what millions of years of erosion can do. At 225 miles (365 km) long, 20 miles (30 km) wide, and nearly 6,000 feet (1,800 meters)

Sea Debris

Rivers dump about 3.5 million tons of loose sand, rocks, plants, and other sediments into the oceans each year.

deep, the canyon has been etched by the Colorado River for more than six million years.

The amount of soil lost through erosion is balanced by the formation of new land. Surface water creates new landforms by carrying away rock, **silt**, and soil and redepositing it in other places. Sometimes **sediment** is carried quite a distance to form land far from where it was originally taken. Unlike the Moon, which has no running water to change its face, Earth's rivers and streams are continually reshaping our landscape.

Humans are disrupting nature's balancing act, however. Normally, plants' roots hold soil in place against the forces of wind and rain, but human activities such as logging, farming, and clearing land destroy the vegetation that keeps erosion in check. People have cut down 60 percent of the world's rain forests. Without a strong root system to hold them in place, the river banks in these areas are easily washed away when the rains come. Too much sediment can clog a river, alter its course, and kill its wildlife. Eventually, whole sections of rain forest look like deserts.

Going Below Ground

While most precipitation evaporates back into the atmosphere or runs off into streams and rivers, about 20 percent of it seeps into the ground. Gravity pulls this **groundwater** down into the **bedrock** below the surface. At shallow depths, in an area called the **zone of aeration**, lies a mixture of rock, air, and water. In this layer, water travels downward at various speeds—anywhere from 1 inch (2.5 cm) to 30 feet (9 m) per day—depending on the **permeability** of the rock, or how quickly water moves through it. Eventually, the water fills up all the pockets and pores in the rock to form the **zone of saturation**. The area between the zones of aeration and saturation is called the **water table**. The water table, our source for groundwater, can be quite close to the ground's surface or hundreds of feet below it.

People drill wells into the water table to pump water to the surface. Well drillers search for an **aquifer**, a layer of permeable rock that contains a large amount of water. Aquifers, which also serve as a major source of springs and rivers, are usually made up of sandstone, gravel, limestone, or basalt—a hard, black volcanic rock. An aquifer can be shallow, less than 50 feet (15 m) below the surface, or as deep as 1,000 feet (300 m) below ground. These natural storage areas can be found under more than half the land in the United States.

Cave Sculptures

Water, combined with carbon dioxide found naturally in air and soil, can eat away at limestone, a common type of bedrock. As it drips in underground caves, the water leaves behind traces of calcium carbonate from the limestone. Drop by drop, the water creates **stalactite** and **stalagmite** jungles like those found in Carlsbad Caverns, New Mexico.

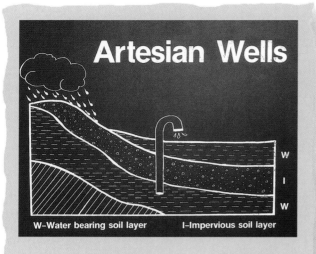

Artesian Hoax

Layers of underground rock sometimes create internal pressure, forcing water to gush out of the ground without being pumped. Despite claims from advertisers, water from these **artesian wells** is no fresher than any other water—but the spurting fountains do put on a good show.

Leaded Pipes

One of the biggest threats to clean water might come from the pipes right in your house. Pipes can leak poisonous lead into drinking water, and, surprisingly, newer homes pose the greatest risk. Since it takes time for mineral deposits in water to form a protective coating in a pipe, a house less than five years old tends to have higher levels of lead in its pipes than an older home does.

Groundwater supplies are especially crucial for cities that get little rainfall, such as those in desert areas. Many aquifers in the Middle East are being drained faster than nature can **recharge**, or refill, them. When this happens, the land can actually sink, or **subside**. When too much water is pumped out, the rock collapses, and the aquifer is destroyed.

In the United States, about half the population uses surface water, while the other half taps into underground aquifers. Whether it is pumped from the ground or already located on the surface, water is stored in **reservoirs**—man-made or natural lakes and ponds. Large rivers, such as the Columbia and the Colorado, are dammed so that their waters can be diverted to reservoirs. From there, the water is used for creating electricity, watering crops, and supplying cities.

Turning on the Tap

For every hundred raindrops that fall, two are likely to find their way to a

faucet. Before it arrives in your home, water from a reservoir must be sent to a treatment plant to be cleaned. At the plant, filtering screens remove mud, dirt, fish, plants, trash, and other objects. Then the water is disinfected to kill bacteria and germs. Some water-treatment plants also spray purified water into the air. This adds more oxygen to improve the water's taste.

The Hoover Dam diverts water from the Colorado River to Lake Mead, a man-made reservoir.

Dam Dilemma

Along the Columbia River in Washington State and Canada, fifty-six major dams block the path salmon take to return to Pacific Northwest waters to spawn, or lay, their eggs. About twenty-five thousand fish manage to navigate home each year, but scientists say that a healthy population should be twice that number.

Water that contains trace amounts of mineral elements, such as calcium, iron, or magnesium, is called **hard water**. It earned this nickname because it is hard to make soap lather in water that is rich in minerals. Hard water is safe to drink, though it can leave stains in your sink and bathtub.

Water is transported to homes and businesses through buried pipes. In some towns, water is stored in elevated tanks high above the buildings they supply. When a tap is opened, the force of gravity moves the water through the pipes. More than 1 million miles (1,600,000 km) of pipes supply water to people in Canada and the United States. That is enough piping to circle the globe forty times.

A Big Gulp

Each day, the United States uses about 400 billion gallons (1.5 trillion L) of freshwater for industry, agriculture, and household consumption. Every American uses about 100–200 gallons (380–750 L) of water each day. Only a small portion of this amount is used for drinking; the rest goes to such things as taking showers, running dishwashers, and watering lawns. In some African countries, where clean water is scarce, the average person's daily use is less than 3 gallons (11 L).

Agriculture swallows most of the world's water, using 65 percent of freshwater supplies to **irrigate**, or water, crops. That leaves only 35 percent to be split among homeowners and industry. In California, crops drink as much as 85 percent of all surface and groundwater.

New technologies are helping decrease the large amounts of water needed to grow food. Through **water recycling**, people use treated wastewater to irrigate crops, golf courses, and parks. Although recycled water is not always purified enough to drink, it is safe for use in paper mills, oil refineries, power plants, flushing toilets, and mixing cement.

Drip irrigation delivers water drop by drop to the root of each plant in a field. Using a tube to water crops individually rather than spraying a whole field saves a great deal of water. Much of the United States, Australia, and Israel (where drip irrigation was invented) now rely on the practice. This slow method of watering crops can be quite expensive, however, which is a major reason why only 1 percent of the world currently uses it.

A drip irrigation system delivers water to individual grape plants in California.

35

Oil washes onshore in Bayonne, New Jersey. Pollution interferes with the delicate balance of the hydrologic cycle and the lives it sustains.

Chapter Five

Troubled Waters

Humans are an important link in the water chain. While the cycle quenches our thirst, we might be the ones to decide its fate—and our own. One-third of the planet's population—nearly two billion people—lacks access to safe drinking water. One of the biggest threats to rivers, lakes, and seas is man-made **pollution**. The most common types of pollution include chemical fertilizers, pesticides, cleaning fluids, radioactive waste, motor oil and gasoline, plastics, and sewage.

Today, more than seventy thousand man-made chemicals are in use around the world, and a thousand new chemicals go on the market each year. These materials are often dumped into rivers, lakes, and streams, where they eventually make their way to the world's oceans. Pollution also puts freshwater supplies in danger, as it seeps into groundwater and poisons aquifers.

Although the vast seas are better able to break down pollution than smaller bodies of water, scientists believe that the oceans are beginning to feel the stress of too much poison. Each year, more than 3 million tons of oil spews into the ocean. Most of it comes from refineries (some oil is deliberately rinsed into the sea when tankers are cleaned), while a small portion is

People push the body of a dolphin out of the Black Sea in Bulgaria. This animal's death, as well as that of ten other dolphins, was attributed to polluted waters of the Danube River.

due to tanker accidents. Between ten and fifteen thousand oil spills occur each year in the United States alone.

In Europe, the once-thriving waters of the Black Sea are all but dead. Sixteen nations unload their waste into the three hundred rivers and streams that flow into the sea. The supply of fish is nearly gone, and filthy beaches are a threat to swimmers. Rivers such as the Danube, which runs into the Black Sea, also suffer from high pollution levels.

Toxic Drops

Raindrops are nature's air cleaner. They bring down much of the pollen, dirt, and gases that are found naturally in the air. When humans send heavy pollution clouds into the sky, the rain changes. Burning **fossil fuels** like coal, oil, and gas releases toxic chemicals such as sulfur dioxide and nitrogen oxides into the air. Water vapor condenses onto these pollutants to form precipitation called **acid rain**.

Factories and industry churn out 91 million tons of nitrogen and sulfur dioxides into the air each year. Automobiles, airplanes, lawn mowers, and other gas-powered machines also choke the air with toxins. As winds carry this pollution around the world, acid rain falls on forests and lakes far from its source.

Acid rain kills plants, frogs, fish, and other wildlife. It can even eat away at the stone in

Acid rain has damaged Cleopatra's Needle, an Egyptian obelisk that currently stands in New York City's Central Park.

bridges and buildings. In Washington, DC, many of our national monuments have been damaged.

Acid rain looks perfectly normal, and the water it pollutes remains crystal clear. It might take years for people to realize that a lake habitat has been **contaminated**, or spoiled. In the United States, one in five lakes has higher than normal acid levels. Waterways in Canada, Scandinavia, central Europe,

Cars of the Future

DaimlerChrysler is working on an electric car powered by oxygen and hydrogen fuel cells. The new car, which should be on the market by 2012, is efficient, easy to recharge, and nonpolluting—it emits only water vapor. The downside? The price. For now, fuel-cell cars cost ten times more than today's standard models.

Dying for Water

More than two hundred cities in China do not have enough water.

In Beijing, one-third of the city's wells have gone dry.

and Asia are also hard hit by acid rainfall. Alternative energy sources such as solar and wind power, along with the search for cleaner-burning fuel, might help combat the effects of acid rain.

A Thirsty World

In the minute it will take you to read this paragraph, 250 babies will be born into the world. On a planet of six billion people, meeting the demand for freshwater is one of the biggest challenges we face. Severe water shortages have already hit China, Africa, and the Middle East, where aquifers and rivers are emptied faster than nature can recharge them.

The Aral Sea in Russia, at 280 miles (448 km) long, was once the fourth-largest body of freshwater in the world. In the 1950s, the former Soviet Union's decision to grow crops in the desert doomed the sea. Farmers tapped the rivers that flowed into the Aral and took so much water that within only a few decades, the sea had shrunk by half. The town of Muynak, once a fishing port, now lies 30 miles (48 km) from the water's edge.

In the United States, the Colorado River is being stretched beyond its limits. Seven states, along with Mexico, dip into the river. Throughout the Southwest, the water is often used for filling swimming pools and watering lawns and golf courses. One-third of the Colorado is tapped by major cities such as Los Angeles, Salt Lake City, and Denver. Dams block much of its natural flow, and in some places the river has gone completely dry. Today, the Colorado River no longer flows to the Pacific Ocean.

Taming Nature

For centuries, humans have tried to read, predict, and even control the weather that delivers our most basic resource: water. "Rainmakers," as they were called, used to travel throughout the hot, dry Midwest promising to bring much-needed water to withering crops—for a price. Though they claimed their secrets would magically unleash a downpour, the

rainmakers did little more than pick the pockets of the farmers who believed them.

Today's **hydrologists**, scientists who study water, have a better handle on what it takes to coax clouds into giving up a few precious drops. Through a process called **cloud seeding**, they scatter silver iodide, dry ice (frozen CO_2), or salt into a cloud to help it form raindrops. Cloud seeding has been somewhat successful, but the process does not work on clouds that lack the necessary moisture.

Science is also turning the tables on nature through **desalinization**, the process of removing salt from ocean water to make it drinkable. Currently, 11,000 desalinization plants

Cloud-seeding planes spray a mixture of dry ice, salt, and other chemicals to induce rain over parched fields in Thailand.

operate in 120 countries, mostly in the Middle East and Africa. Since it requires a lot of energy, however, desalinization is too expensive for many countries that could benefit from it.

Tampa, Florida, is currently building the largest desalinization plant in the western hemisphere. The plant will convert 44 million gallons (167 billion L) of salt water into 25 million gallons (95 billion L) of freshwater daily. It will also spew millions of gallons of the removed brine, or salt, back into the bay. Although many biologists say the plant will be safe, conservationists worry that so much salt will spell disaster for local wildlife and plants.

Water Wars

When survival is at stake, could war break out over water? It has happened before. For a number of thirsty nations, new technologies and conservation might not be enough to offset growing populations that are fast **depleting** water supplies.

More than four thousand years ago, ancient cities battled for rights to the Tigris River. Today, Turkey is building a $32 billion dam on the Tigris. Syria and Iraq, both located downstream, fear that the project will rob them of water. As a result, tensions between the nations are growing.

Egypt, whose population is growing by one million people per year, shares the Nile River with several other African countries. Egypt is the Nile's last stop before it empties into the Mediterranean Sea, and in some places, the river is barely

Drying Up

Hydrologists estimate that if Saudi Arabia continues gulping water at its present rate, the country will completely run out of water within fifty years.

flowing. The Egyptian government is so concerned about water shortages that it has threatened to declare war on any nation that draws too much water from the Nile.

There is hope for global cooperation, however. Jordan and Israel, which compete for dwindling supplies from the Sea of Galilee and the Jordan River, have agreed to try and share water rights. Turkey is considering piping water to nations that need it—for a high price.

In developing countries around the globe, more than one billion people lack access to freshwater. In the next twenty-five years, the number of people living in areas with water shortages is expected to increase by 600 percent. As water supplies dwindle and demand increases, water could become as valuable as diamonds—and perhaps more rare. In a thirsty world, how we protect and restore what nature has given us today will set the course for the water cycle tomorrow.

The Nile River barely flows in Bahr el Ghazal, Sudan. Concerned about water shortages, the Egyptian government is at odds with other countries that share the river.

Teenagers in Austin, Texas, participate in a community lake clean-up project.

Chapter Six

Where Do You Stand?

Before 1900, people used a tiny fraction of Earth's available freshwater supply. Today, we use more than half of it. Unless something changes, many countries will probably run out of water sometime in this century. What can you do?

First, read books and newspapers, and search the World Wide Web to explore the water issues we face. For instance, conservationists want to remove some of the dams that threaten fish such as the sockeye and Chinook salmon. Perhaps you like to fish, and you have noticed that there are fewer salmon in your waters and more restrictions on where you can cast your line. Maybe you feel it is important to protect endangered wildlife.

On the other hand, taking down dams would mean less water in our reservoirs. The price of water could skyrocket, and you might not be able to use as much as you do now. Some people believe that we should not put the environment ahead of our own survival. By becoming informed, you can decide for yourself how best to balance human needs against those of nature.

Second, get involved by conserving water. Here are a few things you can do:

- Turn the tap off while brushing your teeth.
- Limit your shower to less than 10 minutes.
- Repair leaky faucets. A leak of just one drop per second can waste 2,400 gallons (9,000 L) of water over the course of a year.
- Never litter or dump anything toxic, such as paint, pesticides, or motor oil, into storm drains, where poisons can flow into streams and pollute water or kill fish.
- Try to reduce your use of plastic products. Plastic cups, wrappers, and bags can harm wildlife and poison waters.
- Encourage your school to adopt a water-conservation program or organize a clean-up day at a river or beach in your area.

- Contact the U.S. Geological Survey for more information on careers in hydrology: *http://www.usgs.gov*

Opinions differ on how best to use our waterways, but there is agreement on one thing: we must all work together if we are to make sure future generations have plenty of clean, fresh water.

Glossary

acid rain—rain with an abnormally high acid content due to increased levels of pollution in the air

aquifer—an underground layer of rock that stores enough water to be tapped for human use

artesian well—a well in which the water is under enough pressure to force it to the surface without being pumped

atmospheric pressure—the downward pressure exerted by the atmosphere; also called air pressure

bedrock—solid rock, such as limestone, granite, and sandstone, found beneath the soil

climate—the long-term average weather of a particular region over many years

cloud—a visible formation of water droplets or ice crystals in the air

cloud condensation nuclei (CCN)—tiny particles of dirt, dust, clay, salt, pollen, or pollutants onto which water vapor condenses to form clouds

cloud seeding—a process by which chemicals are sprayed into clouds in an attempt to cause rain or snowfall

condense—to change from a gas into a liquid

contaminate—to spoil, make impure

deplete—to use up, decrease

desalinization—the removal of salt from seawater to make freshwater

drip irrigation—a method of irrigation in which pipes slowly drip water onto individual plants

drought—an extended period of time with less than normal rainfall

erode—to wear away

evaporate—to change from a liquid into a gas

fossil fuels—fuels, such as coal, oil, and natural gas, that emit sulfur dioxide and nitrogen oxides, poisonous gases that help create acid rain

freezing point—the temperature at which freshwater turns from a liquid into a solid, 32° F (0° C)

groundwater—water located below the ground's surface

habitat—the environment of a living organism

hard water—water that is rich in traces of minerals, such as calcium or magnesium

humidity—the amount of moisture in the air

hydrologic cycle—the continuous loop of evaporation and precipitation that keeps water traveling from the Earth to the sky and back again

hydrologist—a scientist who studies water

irrigate—to water crops through man-made methods that make up for lack of rainfall

jetstream—a band of high, fast-moving winds that push major weather systems around the globe

El Niño—a cyclical weakening of trade winds that allows the warm waters of the western Pacific Ocean to flow eastward and block the usual flow of cold waters to South America, thereby affecting ocean currents, jetstreams, and weather around the world

permeability—the measure of how easily water flows through rocks

pollution—natural or man-made substances that harm the environment

precipitation—any form of rain, ice, or snow that falls from a cloud

prevailing winds—winds that tend to blow from a particular direction, such as the polar easterlies, the westerlies, and the trades

recharge—to restore or replace, as in a water supply

reservoir—a natural or man-made pond, lake, or basin used to store water

runoff—water that is not absorbed into the ground and instead flows into streams, rivers, lakes, and oceans

sediment—an accumulation of loose pieces of rock and organic material

silt—fine particles of rocks, minerals, and organic materials

stalactite—an icicle-shaped limestone rock, created by dripping water, that hangs from the roof of a cave

stalagmite—an icicle-shaped limestone rock, created by dripping water, that points upward from the floor of a cave

stomata—the tiny pores on leaves through which water transpires

subside—to drop or collapse, as land does when too much groundwater is pumped from an aquifer

surface water—water found on the surface of Earth, including rivers, streams, lakes, ponds, and oceans

transpiration—the process by which water evaporates into the air through the leaves of plants

water molecule (H_2O)—the smallest particle of water, made up of two hydrogen atoms and one oxygen atom

water recycling—the reuse of treated wastewater for purposes other than drinking, such as irrigation and manufacturing

water table—the line between the zone of aeration and the zone of saturation; the source of groundwater for human consumption

water vapor—water in the form of an invisible gas

wind—air that is moving

zone of aeration—the first underground layer of rock, air, and water

zone of saturation—an underground layer of rock whose pores are filled with water

To Find Out More

Books

Arnold, Caroline. *El Niño: Stormy Weather for People and Wildlife*. New York: Clarion, 1998.

Edmonds, Alex. *A Closer Look at Acid Rain*. Brookfield, CT: Millbrook Press, 1997.

Morgan, Sally. *Ecology & Environment: The Cycles of Life*. New York: Oxford University Press, 1995.

Nye, Bill. *Bill Nye the Science Guy's Big Blue Ocean*. New York: Hyperion, 1999.

Walker, Sally. *Water Up, Water Down: The Hydrologic Cycle*. Minneapolis, MN: Carolrhoda, 1992.

Water, the Source of Life. Translated by Jennifer Riggs. New York: Scholastic, 1996.

Videos

Chasing El Niño, NOVA Television, WGBH Boston, 1998.

Eyewitness Weather, Dorling Kindersley Vision, 1996.

CD-ROMs

Exploring Water Habitats, Raintree Steck-Vaughn, 1997.

Science Court: The Water Cycle, Tom Snyder Productions, Watertown, MA, 1997.

Organizations and Online Sites

Center for Marine Conservation
1725 DeSales Street NW, Suite 600
Washington, D.C. 20036
(202) 429-5609
http://www.cmc-ocean.org
This organization seeks to protect ocean and marine environments. The Web site features tips on water conservation, recycling, and keeping the seas clean. You can also fill out a questionnaire to give your school an environmental report card.

The Conservation Fund
Freshwater Institute
P.O. Box 1889
Shepherdstown, WV 25443
(304) 876-2815
http://www.conservationfund.org/conservation/freshwater/
This group is devoted to conserving water resources and developing new technologies.

National Oceanographic and Atmospheric Administration (NOAA)
14th Street & Constitution Avenue
Washington, D.C. 20230
(202) 482-6090
http://www.noaa.gov/
This government organization researches weather, climate, and oceans and provides forecast data for the public through the National Weather Service. Visit the NOAA Web site to learn more about ocean currents and El Niño.

U.S. Environmental Protection Agency
Office of Ground Water and Drinking Water
Ariel Rios Building
1200 Pennsylvania Avenue NW
Washington, D.C. 20460
http://www.epa.gov/kids/
http://www.epa.gov/OGWDW/kids

The EPA sets and enforces water-quality laws in the United States. Check out their Web sites for kids to learn more about the water cycle, pollution, and acid rain.

U.S. Fish and Wildlife Service
1849 C Street NW
Washington, D.C. 20240
http://www.fws.gov/kids
This government agency is dedicated to protecting plants, fish, wildlife, and endangered species. The Web site contains ways your school can preserve rare and threatened animals.

A Note on Sources

When researching a topic as far-reaching as the water cycle, I read as much as possible about the topic. Books such as *Water: A Natural History*, by Alice Outwater, offered a historical perspective, while *Our Poisoned Waters*, by Edward F. Dolan, and *Water Wars*, by Olga Cossi, allowed me to explore the controversies and consequences of water use around the world.

I relied on organizations such as the U.S. Geological Survey and the Environmental Protection Agency for water statistics, information on new technologies, and conservation tips. Videos like NOVA's *Chasing El Niño* and the BBC-Timelife *Living Plant* series added further dimension to the topic.

Newspapers and magazines rounded out my research, bringing to light current events and concerns such as pollution and worldwide water shortages.

—*Trudi Strain Trueit*

Index

Numbers in *italics* indicate illustrations.

About the Author

As a weather forecaster for KREM (CBS) TV in Spokane, Washington, and KAPP TV (ABC) in Yakima, Trudi Strain Trueit has traveled to schools throughout the Pacific Northwest to share the world of weather with elementary and middle-school students. She is the author of three other Watts Library Earth Science books: *Clouds*, *Storm Chasers*, and *Rain, Hail, and Snow*.

An award-winning television news reporter, Trueit has contributed stories to ABC News, CBS News, CNN, and the Speedvision Channel. Trueit, who has a B.A. in broadcast journalism, is a freelance writer and journalist. She lives in Everett, Washington, with her husband, Bill.